PENNY STOCKS

All You Need To Know To Invest Intelligently in Penny Stocks

JONATHAN S. WALKER

DEDICATION

I dedicate this book to my two beautiful children and my loving wife who have been nothing short of being my light and joy throughout the years.

herein.

Additionally, the information in the following pages is intended only for informational purposes and should thus be thought of as universal. As befitting its nature, it is presented without assurance regarding its prolonged validity or interim quality. Trademarks that are mentioned are done without written consent and can in no way be considered an endorsement from the trademark holder.

VIP Subscriber List

Dear Reader, If you would like to receive latest tips and tricks on internet marketing, exclusive strategies, upcoming books & promotions, and more, do subscribe to my mailing list in the link below! I will be giving away a free book that you can download right away as well after you subscribe to show my appreciation!

Here's the link: http://bit.do/jonathanswalker

CONTENTS

Introduction

Congratulations on purchasing your personal copy of *Penny Stocks: All You Need To Know To Invest Intelligently.* Thank you for doing so.

The following chapters will discuss some of the many things that you are able to do in order to grow your investment and to start making six figures in no time. The guidebook will start with some information on penny stocks, such as what penny stocks are, some of the best strategies to do well in penny stocks and how to pick the stocks that will help you to make the best decision to make money even as a beginner.

Next, we will move on to learning about some of the other investment opportunities that you can choose from t make a lot of money. We will talk about some of the basics of picking out an investment, the different types that you can pick such as bonds, the stock market, and real estate, and then some of the strategies that you can use no matter what investment you choose to go with.

When it is time to make your money grow and you want to replace your regular income, investing is the option for you. Take a look through this guidebook and learn some of the basics that you need to know about penny stocks, as well as some of the other investment types so that you can start making money today!

Part 1: Penny Stocks

Chapter 1: What are Penny Stocks?

Penny stocks are relatively simple, but there are a few tricks that you need to learn in order to make them work for your needs. They represent stocks that are going to have a low price, usually a price that is under a dollar, as well as a smaller market cap that is under $500 million. For the most part, when an investor is working with penny stocks, they are going to be traded off of the traditional exchanges, so you will not find them on the New York Stock Exchange or on the NASDAQ.

So why would you want to choose to work with penny stocks rather than another investment type? There are several reasons to use penny stocks, but they are often used in order to help a company procure the right capital so that the company can grow and become more powerful. Through this market, the company is able to build up the money that is needed so they can grow their business and when you pick the right company, they can make a strong investment for a low cost.

Penny stocks are going to be traded in order to benefit some of the smaller public companies. But if this company does well, and you purchased the stock over the counter before it entered the regular stock exchanges, you could get a great return on investment. Even if the company never makes it over to the regular stock exchange, many of these can still increase their profits and you can earn back on your investment.

Almost all of the penny stocks are going to be sold on over the counter exchanges. This is going to work because many of the larger exchanges are going to have stringent policies before a company can join them and trade. Most of the companies that are in penny stocks will come nowhere near reaching these stringent requirements, plus it costs a lot of money to trade on these exchanges, so it isn't possible for some smaller companies to make it work. Instead of trying to meet some of these requirements or come up with large amounts of money that they don't have, the companies are going to work with the penny stocks to get the funding they need. As the investor, you are able to capitalize on this and get some great stocks, often from some growing companies, for a low price.

As the investor, you need to remember that there will be some risk that comes with going with penny stocks. If you take the time to educate yourself and learn how to avoid some of the major mistakes that come with this investment, you are more likely to make a good income in the process, but keep in mind there are some risks and they are sometimes seen as speculative in nature, rather than as an investment.

Benefits of going with penny stocks

First, let's take some time to look at the benefits of going with penny stocks. Penny stocks could be your next big break. They are a lot of fun to work with because there are a lot of companies who are out there and are looking to use penny stocks as a way to raise capital to grow and become big. If you pick out the right company, you could be one of the first people in on it, and that stock that you got for under a dollar will end up being worth a lot of money down the road if the company does grow.

That is one of the main benefits that come with investing is that there is the potential of making a huge return on investment. You need to make sure that you purchase a stock that is at a low price, which is easy to do in penny stocks, and make sure that it has a good business plan and will survive the market, just like you would with any other investment, and you will see results. Not all companies that are in penny stocks will make it to the big leagues, but many of them can still grow and you can make money from this process.

Many investors like to go with penny stocks because they are exciting and a lot of fun to work with. It is fun and can feel great, to start out with a little bit of money and then move up and see it grow. You may not make a ton of money at first, but penny stocks can help you to start with a small investment and get it to grow. If you want to start out your portfolio and you don't have a ton of money for it, penny stocks can be a great place to start.

The negatives of penny stocks

One of the first negatives that you should be aware of when you are working in penny stocks is that many of the companies on the market are not that good. There are some companies who are really good and just need to make a few tweaks or make a bit more profit before they are able to join the regular stock markets. But many of the companies that you will find in penny stocks didn't get onto the major stock exchanges because they were just bad. You need to learn how to tell the difference between the two if you would like to make an income here.

In addition, the penny stock market is not as reliable as the major stock markets. They are unreliable and they often don't have regulations in place to determine which companies or transactions that go on with them. This doesn't mean that all of the companies are bad on the penny stock market, but since there aren't really a lot of regulations that are in place, many bad companies can sneak through, make up numbers, or hide information and it is really risky picking out the company you want to work with. You will need to be diligent and really do your research to make sure that you are picking out good companies that will earn you money over time.

Penny stocks are really interesting investments to make. They usually have stocks that come in under a dollar each, so they are a good choice for those who have limited money to invest with in the beginning. While you do need to be on guard against some of the bad companies that are able to get onto the penny stock exchange, there are still many great ones that are available that you can pick from and that will help you to make a good return on your investment!

Chapter 2: Picking the Right Trading Strategies

When it comes to working in penny stocks, or any other investment for that matter, one of the most important things that you will need to do is figure out the strategy that you want to use. The strategy is so important because it is going to determine which stocks you will purchase when you will purchase them and sell them, and what research you will do to get the results. There are many great strategies that are available and none of them are necessarily any better or worse than the others, but you will find that picking a strategy and sticking with it, rather than bouncing back and forth between a few, can make all the difference. Some of the best trading strategies that you can use when you want to trade in penny stocks include:

Scalping

This is often a popular strategy to go with because it is pretty simple to use and many beginners like this simplicity. With the idea of scalp trading, you are going to take advantage of some of the inefficiencies that are going on in the market with respect to the spread. The gap between the bid price and the asking price, which is known as the spread, can end up widening or narrowing rapidly throughout time, and even through the day and they are going to create some great selling and buying opportunities that will result in some quick profits.

To scalp, you will need to be good at watching the market and understanding the perfect time to purchase and sale. You can even look at a few markets and see if you are able to find the stocks of a company a little lower than the price of them on the other. You would then purchase the stock at the lower price before moving it over to the other market and selling it for the higher price that is demanded there. You can end up selling the stocks pretty quickly this way and while the profit may only be a little bit on each one, if you purchase quite a few stocks and do this many times, you can make a good profit.

Range trading

When things are going along as normal and all of the other things in the market are even, stocks are often going to trade inside of a set trading range each day. When you use range trading to help you to purchase and sell your penny stocks, you will try to purchase the stock when it is at the bottom of the range, and then when it gets to the top, you will want to sell it. To do this type of trading, you will want to make sure that the stocks have a consistent trading range each day so that you can make some good estimates.

So with this one, you are going to take a look at some of the history of the company, if it is available, and find out what places seem to be the high points of the stock and which ones seem to be the low points. There can be some variations of this each day, but mostly you will notice that the trend stays about the same. You will then take this information to help you make the right purchases on all of your stocks. You will be able to make a purchase of the stock when the market is at the low end of the range and then you can sell the stock when it goes back up before it goes down and you lose out again. This one will require you to spend some time looking through many graphs and charts to get the information, but it can be pretty straightforward and can make you a good profit.

Momentum trading

This is the trading option that you will go with if you are looking to go with some of the trends that are in the market to make a good profit. In basic terms, you are going to use momentum trading or trend trading to purchase a stock when it is trending up, but then you will sell the stock as soon as the trend starts to go back down. This one can be a little less risky compared to some of the others, but you have to constantly be watching the trends and the market to make sure that you get out before all of your investment is gone.

Real-time new trading.

Another option that you are able to go with when

you are working on penny stocks is known as real time news trading. This is the one where you are going to have to spend some time reading or watching the news and looking for some clues as to how a market or a particular company is going to do. When you find that some good news is released, you will make the purchase, and then after that little punch up, you will sell the stock. It can also work to protect your investment because if you notice that some bad news is about to happen, you can sell the stocks without losing all the money, and then purchase them again when things settle down.

If you want to use this kind of trading strategy, you will want to make sure that you download a real-time news feed so that you are always getting information in. You also need to be able to understand what each piece of news can mean to the penny stocks that you are working with. You don't want to misunderstand what is going on and end up with selling a stock that was going up or losing out on a stock because you held onto it for too long.

When it comes to picking out the strategy that you want to use for your penny stocks, you will find that there is really no wrong answer. Each person is going to pick out a different strategy to help them out, and what works for one person is not going to work for you. Make sure to check out some of these strategies and then pick the one that works the best for you!

Chapter 3: Getting Started with Your First Trade

When you are ready to get started with your first trade in penny stocks, you will need to take a couple of steps. First, it is important to figure out the broker that you would like to work with. there are many different brokers available out there and many of them have great reputations that can help you to get done with your trading. You should compare a few of them right from the beginning, looking at the features that they offer, as well as some of the fees and costs that they will hand down to you. These will all affect how easy it is to do trades with your broker and how much you will actually make.

Once you have chosen the broker you want to work with, it is time to pick the strategy that you want to work with as well. There are many different strategies, and we discussed a few of them in the chapter above. These can all be successful based on what you would like to get out of the trading. The most important option here is to learn about the different trading strategies for penny stocks and then stick with it.

Many of the investors who end up failing are the ones who just can't seem to stick with the trading strategy that they originally picked. These are the people who will bounce back and forth between a few different options, but they never get familiar or comfortable with just one of them. You can pick any of the strategies that you would like, but you need to make sure that you are sticking with it if you want to see results.

Next on the list is to choose the stocks that you would like to invest in. This is the part that is going to take some time and you will probably need to use your chosen strategy to help you make the right decisions. When you are picking a stock to invest in, especially when it comes to the penny stock market, you want to make sure that you are being really careful. This is a fantastic market to get into, but if you are not paying attention and doing your research, you will find that your money will be all gone. Many good companies get onto the penny stock market, but so do many bad ones so you have to be diligent if you want to see success.

There are a number of things that you can do to make sure you pick out the right stocks when working in the penny stock market. First, make sure to check out the numbers on your own. Most companies want to gain your trust and will put up their sales information and other relevant things to help you make a good decision to go with them. But since this is not always required of stocks on the penny stock market, there are some that may not provide this information at all and some that will hide factors or fudge the numbers a bit. Doing your own research, and being critical to see if that research is correct, can be a great way to ensure that you are picking out good stocks that will help you earn money.

Always be critical when it comes to picking out a stock on this market. There are too many new investors who are excited to get into the trading business and who want to be able to pick out a company that will make it big. But if you jump in too quickly and don't pay attention to what you are doing while trading, you are going to end up in trouble, and probably losing a lot of money. Make smart decisions, pick out stocks that you think will do well, and always go through and do your own research, and you are sure to see the results.

And finally, after you have chosen your strategy and the stocks that you want to invest in, you have to decide how much you want to invest. Since the penny stock market is often inexpensive, with many of the options coming in at under a dollar, it is pretty affordable for you to make some purchase and get started. But even so, you will want to set the maximum that you want to spend on the stocks, as well as how much you are willing to lose before you get out of the market. Having this plan in place ahead of time can help you to make informed decisions, rather than ones attached to your emotions, and you will see much less risk in the process.

Along the way, if you happen to have any questions about how things are working or what you should do, turning to your broker can be a great idea. They have a lot of experience working in the various investments so they should be able to answer any of the questions or the concerns that come up and they can lead you in the right direction to making a good return on your investment.

Part 2: Investors Ultimate Guide from Novice to Expert

Chapter 4: The Basics of Investing

Many people are interested in investing, but they are not sure what steps to take to get started. Many times the information that is available can be confusing and once they enter the market, it is just too much to handle. Luckily, investing doesn't have to be hard, you just need to understand how to get started. Let's take a look at some of the basics that come with investing so that you can get started.

What is investing?

first, investing is going to refer to business activities where an investor will spend money in order to gain a profit. The investment is supposed to help the investor to make money and increase the value of their money through some business activities. There are many different ways that you can do this. You can choose to start your own business and invest funds into that, you can invest in the stock market, you can choose real estate investing, and so much more. But whatever type of investment that you choose, there needs to be at least some chance of making the money back and even making a profit, otherwise, it is too risky to work with.

All of the methods above are great ways to help invest your money, you simply need to pick the one that works the best for you. You should also spend some time learning how to reduce the risk of your investment. For example, if you wanted to start a business, you would learn about the market, make a good product, and find ways to sell the product so that you can make a good profit without losing out on all of your money. If you just go into an investment without some planning, you are basically gambling rather than investing.

Before you decide to get into an investment, it is a good idea have a little bit of savings ready to go. If you make smart decisions on your investment, you shouldn't have too many issues with losing all of your money, but some investments, such as real estate, can be labor and time intensive and having some savings in hand ahead of time can reduce the risk and help reduce the stress. Then when you start to invest, make sure that a few your profits go back into your savings to help out as well.

In addition, this savings can be a great way to get started on your investment. Most of us don't have a ton of extra money lying around that we can use for this kind of investment. But if we take a few months and put a little bit back for savings, it is easier to reach our goals. Then we are able to start investing without having to cut into our income or the money that we need to pay our bills when first starting out.

Before you are able to get into a new investment you need to pick out which one you would like to go with. There ae so many different options and part of the fun is figuring out which one is the right one to match up with your skills and interest levels. If you are interested in starting your own business, you can go with that investment, but other people may be interested in working in real estate and flipping houses or renting them out. Some people want to just invest their money with a friend or family member who is starting up something, and others like to work in the different parts of the stock market. All of these have the potential of being good investments, you just need to pick one and learn how it works!

Getting started in investing is a great way to make your money work for you. There are different options and all of them are going to require you to pick out different strategies to make them work. But when you are able to do this, you can make a good income from your investment.

Chapter 5: The Different Investing Options

So, in order to be successful with investing, you need to pick out the investment opportunity that works the best for you. There are a number of options that you can pick from, but as a beginner, you will probably want to start out with just one option. Yes, there are those investors who seem to have their hands in almost every market that is out there, but this can take some time to build up and as a beginner, that is going to be way too much for you to handle. If you are still considering which type of investment you want to work with and you aren't sure where to start, check out some of these options to help make the decision easier.

The stock market

The first place that people think about when they

are working on investments is the stock market. The stock market is basically a platform where shares of companies can be bought and also sold. The shares are going to be units of ownership in the company and when you purchase one of these shares, you become one of the owners of the company. Just like a traditional owner, you will be entitled to parts of the assets as well as the future profits of the company. So if the company grows and does well, you will make an income for holding onto the shares.

A common mistake with this is that new investors assume that they should purchase as many shares as they can to make a good profit. This can be one method to make a profit, but professional investors will agree that it is best to purchase stocks that have the potential to grow. You are going to make a bigger profit from 50 shares that go up to $100 each compared to 100 shares that go up to $2 each, even if you ended up purchasing them for the same total price.

There are many options when it comes to investing in the stock market. Some people choose to pick a company to invest in for the long-term and will hold onto the stock, earning a profit each quarter as long as the company does well. Day trading is popular as well and it includes you purchasing and selling the stock all on the same day to make a bunch of little profits that add up. You can also choose from forex trading, options trading, and penny stocks as well. Each of these have their own unique set of rules and own risks so make sure that you fully understand them before starting.

The bond market

Another investment type is to work with the bond market. With this option, you are taking on less risk and you know right from the beginning how much you will earn in interest, but the return on investment is lower than the stock market or other options. In the bond market, the government and other companies are looking to borrow money from investors to expand their business or to do other things to help them grow. The investor will be able to lend out this money in the form of a band, and the company or the government can then use it for their plans.

With the bond, you will invest a certain amount of money that you are not allowed to take out again until the maturity date of the bond. Sometimes this will be a few months but it can go for several years. You will get to determine the maturity date that you are comfortable with before you start. The bond will have an interest rate attached to it, which is the amount that the investor will earn on their investment when the maturity date hits. It is a safe and secure way to make a little bit of money on your investment and can help you to grow your portfolio without all the risk that is found with some of the other options.

Investing in commodities

Some investors like to invest in commodities to see a profit. Commodities are going to refer to produce that is high in demand and also publicly traded. The products themselves will not be traded on this market. The speculators and the investors in this market are going to contract for the future value of the product. Let's look at an example of coffee. Many countries will produce coffee and this can be a great commodity to work with.

With this system, you are going to pick the commodity that you want to work with and then sign a future contract for the amount that you will spend, say $100,000. If the price of the coffee goes up by the end date, you will be able to get a profit. But if for some reason the price of the coffee goes down, you will lose the money. You need to have a good idea of the market for the commodity that you want to work with and be able to estimate what is going to happen with it in the future in order to make money with this option.

Foreign exchange

Working with foreign currencies is another option that is available for a trader. With this option, you are going to make a purchase of another currency, perhaps the GBP, when the price is relatively low compared to the American one. Then you will wait until it is worth more in the future, and change it back over to the USD, making a profit in the process. For example, if you changed over to the GBP when it was worth $1.2 USD, and then held onto it for a bit until 1 GBP was worth $1.5 USD, you would make a profit of $0.30 on every dollar that you spent, which can add up if you did a larger investment.

This was traditionally a method that was only used by the banks and governments of different countries, but it is now an option that many different people are able to use thanks to the newer technology. You do need to be careful with this option though because the currency market is always fluctuating and you never know if your money is going to be worth more or less in the future. But if you are able to hold onto the money for some time and can watch the exchange rates, you can make a good profit from this option.

Starting your own business

Some people choose to start their own business in order to start a new investment. There are many options that you can choose, from brick and mortar stores to working from home. But no matter what kind of business you decide to start, you will have to put some money forward to get started. For example, even if you want to be a writer from home, you will need to invest in a good computer, some writing software, the internet, and even some storage to help keep files in order. If you want to start a clothing store, you would need to rent out a building, purchase the clothes, hire employees, and so on.

There is quite a bit of risk that can happen with starting a business, but if you think it all out, come up with a good business plan and stick with it, you can start to make a good profit from your own business. Plus, you are able to work for yourself, instead of being stuck with a boss, so it can be very appealing to many people.

The real estate market

Many people like to work with the real estate market because this is a market that is often going up. There are some different options that you are able to use when it comes to working in the real estate market, which can make this even more popular since you get to choose the one that works for you. One option that works well with real estate is flipping houses. With this option, you will purchase a home when it is really low in price, perhaps as a foreclosure or when the market is really low. Then you will make some changes to the home, fix it up and make it look nice, and then when the market starts to go up, or when the value is higher, you will sell it to make a profit.

If you are looking to get a more continuous form of income from real estate, you can choose to purchase a home and rent it out. Your rental fees should be enough to cover the cost of the home (or the mortgage) as well as the taxes, maintenance and for you to make a little bit of income. Over time, you can add in a few different properties so that you can make a full-time income in the process.

In addition, there are a lot of options that fall into

the different categories. For example, working with rentals can include single family homes, duplexes, and apartment buildings and you can even work with commercial real estate as well. It all depends on the amount of work that you would like to put into the investment and how much money that you would like to earn.

As you can see, there are quite a few different options that you can pick from when it comes to working on an investment. All of these have the potential to bring you a lot of income, but you just need to pick out the one that meets your interests and that you will enjoy doing the most. Pick out your investment, and you are sure to see a great income in no time!

Chapter 6: The Best Investment Strategies

The next thing that you need to focus on, after you have been able to pick what kind of investment that you would like to work on, is to pick a good strategy that will help you to get this all going. There are a lot of investment types and all of them are going to work in a slightly different manner, so once you pick the investment option, you will need to look a bit more in depth to see what strategies are the most effective for you. But no matter what kind of investment you go with, there are a few strategies that will work for all of them including.

Buy low and sell high

In all of the investments that you work with, the goal is to purchase your asset at the lowest price that you can. If you purchase the investment at a price that is too high, you are going to lose out or not make very much money in the process. You are going to need to work on learning the market in order to understand when is the best time to make the purchase.

When it comes to the stock market, you will want to wait for the market to go down a bit, or at least a dip in the company that you are working with. This will allow you to purchase the stock at a lower price than usual, and then you just need to hold onto the stocks for a bit of time until the market goes up. Of course, you need to learn the difference between a stock being low priced because of the market and it being low priced because the company is failing.

You can use this in other investments as well. When it comes to working with real estate, you will want to look for a downturn in the housing market to get a good discount on the homes you want to purchase and then wait until the market goes back up and you can sell the home for a much higher price. The good news with real estate is that you can rent out the home, and make some income in the process, while you wait for the market to go back up.

No matter what kind of market you get into, you must make sure that you are purchasing the asset at the lowest price possible. This will ensure that your risks are lower and your profits higher. If you aren't good at reading the market and working on your strategy, you will find that you will purchase the asset at a high price and that it will be very difficult to sell it again without taking a loss. The lower that you can get the asset, without picking one that is already failing, the better off you will be when it comes to making a profit.

Be an expert in your market

The idea behind this strategy is that you stay inside just a few markets. You may look at the list of investing options above and feel that you should jump into all of them, but when you generalize in everything, you are setting yourself up for failure. As a beginner, you need to just stick with one option. This allows you to devote your time and energy to this, without becoming overwhelmed. Over time, as you become an expert in that market, you can expand out a little bit and try a few other options, but you should really just concentrate on one at a time and even when you expand, keep the markets similar.

For example, if you want to go into real estate, you should consider working first in renting out single family homes. Do that for a bit of time until you become comfortable with what you are doing and then you can consider expanding your portfolio to not only rent out these single-family homes but to also expand out to renting out duplexes and some small apartment buildings. You are still within the same field, but you are growing your income and diversifying your portfolio all at the same time.

If you are working in the stock market, you can take kind of the same approach. You may start out with a long-term investment in a few stocks, but then over time, you may decide to add some Forex trading or some penny stocks to the mix to help diversify and make more money. You are still working in the stock market, or something similar to it though, so you can take your knowledge and expand it out to other investments.

The thing that you need to watch out for with these investments is skipping from one to another. If you have been doing real estate, you may find that it is hard to jump over to the stock market and going from the stock market to the real estate market can be tough as well, because they are really two different types of investments. Some people have been able to do it, but it is tough and you may find that it is too much to put onto your plate. It is better to just stick with the one market, become an expert in it, and then diversify within it to see the profits that you want.

Pick out financial safe havens

After you learn a bit about how to invest into the stock market or another market for investing, you may want to learn a bit about financial safe havens. These are places where you are able to transfer your money during an economic downturn and which are less likely to be negatively impacted by the market. You would put your money over to these in order to avoid losses, at least until the economy comes back around. Ideally, your safe haven is going to be able to at least beat off inflation so you will still have the same spending power later on.

There are several different types of instruments that you can use for this, but gold is one of the most popular ones. Big investors will often move their money over to gold when the economy gets tough, and this is why you will see that the price of gold will start to climb when markets like stocks and bonds start to do poorly. Gold is not the only safe haven that you can pick. In bearish markets also see a rise in treasury bills, but gold is still the most popular because the interest rates are so low on these treasury bills.

Invest actively

If you are able to get started with a larger sum of money, you are able to start investing in an active manner in the market that you choose. In order to use this particular strategy, you must learn how to become an expert in the chosen industry and focus your energy on these in order to better learn these markets and to make some of the best decisions possible to grow your money.

For example, if you are using this type of strategy, you may want to spend some time reading up on the news of any company that you are interested in investing with. In addition, you would take some time to look at the financial statements of the company, check into their management, and find out if they are growing consistently and are actually a company that you want to work with.

There are thousands of companies who are on the stock exchange and it is important that you learn how to be an active investor. Sure, you could hand over the money to a broker and hope things go well, but the most successful investors are the ones who do the research and pick out the strategy that they want to use on their own. There is nothing wrong with talking to a broker and getting some advice, but you should never let them do all of the work for you.

Focus on the goals

Before you enter into any of the investment types, you should sit down and have some clear cut goals. You want to have a purpose behind your investing and what you want to do if you are actually successful. This will help you to create a system that will lead you to meet this goal. Some people will invest in order to make some side money to help them out with bills and other things, some want to put that money towards retirement and to help them build up a little nest egg. Others are tired of working a regular job and want to be able to work for themselves. Having these goals will help you to see that success, no matter what it is.

For example, if you are looking to make this into an investment into your retirement, you may be more likely to look for long-term investment opportunities that will help you to earn a little bit over each month. If you want to make this into a full-time income, you are going to be more interested in things like flipping homes or riding some of the big waves of the stock market so you can make this income. As you can see, these are very different options of investing, but it always depends on the goals that you are trying to reach for which one you will choose.

So before you decide to go and purchase your asset or get into your chosen market, you need to sit down and decide what your goals are going to be for that investment. Then you can write down the plan that you want to follow in order to make these goals a reality. It is nice to have dreams and to hope that the investment asset that you choose will help you to get there, but if you don't plan ahead and make sure that you have the right strategy, you are never going to see the results that you want.

It is so much you are able to do when it comes to picking out an investment and seeing it grow. Picking out a good strategy will help you to really see the success that you are looking for because it leads you to pick the right asset and making decisions that will make you successful. No matter what kind of investment you choose to go with, make sure to follow some of these simple strategies and you are sure to see some of the success that you are looking for.

PART 2

CHAPTER 1: UNDERSTANDING OPTIONS TRADING

Options trading, also known as *binary options trading,* is just like forex and stock trading. However, you do not need to buy currencies or stocks. Instead, you simply predict whether the value of an underlying asset will increase or decrease at a specified time. It is this simplicity of options trading that attract so many investors. It is an option contract that has a fixed payout.

Options trading vs. forex and stock trading

In forex and stocking trading, you buy currencies or stocks and sell them for profit. In options trading, you do not need to buy any trading asset. You only predict whether the price of an underlying asset will be higher or lower than its current price at the expiration date. Also, in forex and stock trading, your profit will depend on the increase in the value of a particular currency or stock that you have purchased. In options trading, the potential profit is fixed and is revealed to you even before you commence a trade.

It is not uncommon for forex and stock traders to wait for weeks and months just to see a little profit from their investment. Many times, they even lose their investment without any chance of getting any profit. This happens when the price of their stocks or currency drops. With options trading, there is always a potential to earn a big amount of profit even when the price of an underlying asset decreases. You do not have to wait for weeks or months; you can double, or even triple, your investment in a few minutes.

Options trading vs. gambling

There are similarities between options trading and gambling. In some jurisdictions, options trading is literally considered gambling. Just like the casino game called *baccarat* where you decide whether the winning hand is *banker* or *player*, in options trading, you will decide whether the value of an underlying asset will rise (Call) or fall (Put) at the expiration time. Just like the table games in the casino, there is a fixed payout for a favorable outcome.

You might be wondering, "Is options trading gambling?" It depends. If you do options trading by relying on guesswork and pure luck, then you are gambling. However, if you consider every wager that you make an investment decision and take the serious effort to study the market and research the different underlying assets being traded, then you are an investor or trader.

It does not really matter whether you see yourself as a gambler or a trader. In the end, what matters is how much profit you have made, if any.

The Basics

Let us move on to the specific parts of options trading. Do not worry; options trading is very easy. You can learn the basics in less than five minutes. It is only like speculating the outcome of a coin flip.

Call vs. Put

There are only two main options to choose from. In options trading, you just have to know whether the outcome will be a *Call* or a *Put*. Simple, right?

Choose the Call option if you predict that the price of an underlying asset will be *above* its current price at the expiration date.

Choose the Put option if you predict that the price of an underlying asset will be *below* its current price at the expiration date.

These two terms are referred to by many names, depending on the trading platform that you use. They are also known as Up/Down, Above/Below, Rise/Fall, and others.

Strike price

This refers to the price at which an asset can be bought or sold at a certain time. In options trading, this simply refers to the Call or Put option. The Call option is the value at which the underlying asset can be bought, while the Put option is when it can be sold at a specified time.

Expiration time

The expiration time, or simply expiry time, signifies the end of a trading period. This is also the time when you can determine whether or not you have made the right investment decision. Therefore, this is the moment when you will experience a profit or a loss.

In-the-money vs. out-the-money

In-the-money is a *win*. It means that you have made

the right investment decision and earned a profit. On the contrary, out-the-money means that you have lost your wager.

Long-term option

In options trading, you get to choose how long a trade will last (expiration date). A long-term option simply refers to a trade that is long as 24 hours or more. A long-term option can last for a day, weeks, and months.

Speed option

As the name already implies, speed options are trades that last for a short period of time. This can be as fast as 30 seconds, a minute, or up to five to fifteen minutes, depending on the platform that you use.

Assets

Assets are valuable financial instruments. In options trading, you do not have to purchase any asset, you just have to determine if the value of an asset will be greater than or lower than its current price at the expiration time.

When trading binary options, the following assets are traded:

- stocks
- index
- commodities
- currency pairs

Bear market vs. bull market

On the one hand, a bear market means that the prices of certain assets are decreasing or are about to decrease. On the other hand, a bull market means that the prices of certain assets are increasing or are about to increase.

Take note, however, that even though a bear market is considered a negative sentiment, it does not affect you as a trader. In fact, you can even profit from it. This is because options trading has a dual nature: You can make a good amount of profit whether the price of certain underlying assets increase or decrease, provided you choose the right option (Call vs. Put).

Brokers and trading platforms

Before you can start trading binary options, you need to open an account with a broker. You can find many brokers when you make a search online. However, you need to choose a broker that will best suite your needs. Unfortunately, there are also scammers out there, so it is best to work only with a broker that has a well-established reputation.

Here is a list of trusted brokers. Take note that trading platforms may change their policies and management team. Therefore, even the most trusted brokers may no longer be a good choice tomorrow. Before you open an account, check the latest ratings and reviews given by other traders.

- iq option (www.iqoption.com)
- OptionRobot (www.optionrobot.com)
- Automated   Binary (www.automatedbinary.com)
- Finpari (www.finpari.com)
- 24option (www.24option.com)
- fortuneJack (www.fortunejack.com) *bitcoin casino with binary options*

Important note:

Be sure to check the *banking options*. Many brokers accept many methods to make a deposit but only have limited options for making a withdrawal.

CHAPTER 2: RISKS & BENEFITS

Like any business venture, there are a number of risks and benefits associated with options trading. Here are the things that you can expect:

Market risk

The market is composed of real people. This is why it is extremely volatile. And, although there are methods that have been developed to predict market movements, there is no guaranteed way to determine how the market responds.

Lack of ownership

In options trading, you only wager on the future valuation of an underlying asset. Therefore, you do not exercise any right of ownership over any stock or asset.

High-risk investment

Like any other business that offers a high reward, the risk involved is also high. Unlike in trading stocks where you get to keep a losing stock with an opportunity that its price will soon increase or at least sell the stock to cut down your losses, you do not get to keep anything if you encounter a loss in options trading. In options trading, when you lose a trade, you lose the whole amount that you wager on that particular trade.

Limited opportunity

In options trading, the potential payout is already fixed even before you commence a trade. You cannot get a profit higher than the fixed payout. In forex or stock trading, the potential profit is almost limitless.

No liquidity

There is no liquidity because you do not have ownership of the stock or asset being traded. When you commence a trade, you just have to wait for the trading period to end and hope for the best. However, liquidity should not be an issue. After all, there are trades that can last for just a day, even less.

Losing is normal

Although there are people who rake in serious profits with options trading, the majority of traders lose their money, and they lose it within a short period of time.

If your entrepreneurial spirit remains strong and convinced despite the risks that you will encounter along your journey, then it is time for you to know the notable benefits of options trading.

The Benefits

High Return

For those who engage in forex or stock trading, a 50% is already considered high. And, usually, they would have to wait for months just to get a 50% profit. Most of the time, they do not even reach 50%. With options trading, getting a 90% per trade is normal. You can double your money in less than an hour.

Simplicity

It is the beautiful simplicity of options trading that makes it very attractive. You do not need to have any trading portfolio or any gambling experience. You can learn and start earning money with options trading almost instantly.

Fixed payout

Unlike other investment opportunities where you do not know how much money you can make, options trading lets you know the exact amount that you can profit before you commence a trade.

Quick turnover rate

Options trading allows you to choose just how long you want a trade to last. With speed trading, you can make multiple trades in less than five minutes.

Asset variety

Since you do not have to purchase any asset or currency, you have all the available underlying assets to choose from. Also, the minimum amount per trade is usually low, so you can easily diversify the assets that you invest in.

Controlled risk

You do not have to worry about hidden charges or surcharges. Whatever amount that you spend for a particular trade is your total risk. If you just want to risk $100, then simply invest $100, and there is nothing else that you should worry about.

Instant trading

Most established brokers offer a mobile phone feature. This will allow you to manage your account and commence a trade anytime and anywhere.

CHAPTER 3: STRATEGIES

Most people who lose their money with options trading either have no strategy at all and just rely on pure luck, or have a poor and underdeveloped strategy. If you want to rake in serious profits with options trading, you need to have a solid strategy. Unlike casino games where you simply have to vary the amount of your bets, success in options trading requires serious research, analysis, and practice.

Fundamental analysis

Fundamental analysis is considered the lifeblood of investment. This is the key to increasing your chances of making a profit. Remember that the market is run by real people and businesses, In fundamental analysis, you need to gather various information and analyze the economy, financial statements of businesses, as well as the latest news, among others. By analyzing these data, you can come up with a better investment decision. For example, if there is a report that the problem of the high unemployment rate has just been resolved in the U.S., and all other things being normal, then you can expect the value of the U.S. currency to increase.

If you like numbers, then fundamental analysis is the way to go. However, it is not recommended for speed options. This is because economic and business changes take time. It is best to use this method for trades that last for more than 12 hours.

Technical analysis

If you do not like analyzing lots of numbers, then technical analysis may be for you. Technical analysis is more visual. You will be analyzing charts and graphs. Technical analysis is excellent for fast trading or speed options. The proper way to use this method is to view the available graphs and look for patterns.

A note about patterns: Patterns depend on the latest trend. Is it a bull or a bear market? The risk here is that trends are not permanent. They change —and they usually change quickly. The key here is to find a pattern and be able to place your wager just before the trend changes.

Algorithmic and signals

By using computer programs and apps that can be installed on your computer, you will know where to invest in. This is an easy and quick way to come up with a decision; however, this method is not recommended because it is unreliable. There is simply no computer program that can accurately read the market's movement. However, this can be useful as secondary information.

Co-integration trading

This strategy uses the correlation that is created between two underlying assets. This usually occurs when two assets are in the same industry or have the same market. Due to their high correlation, you will notice that their prices are always close to each other. Hence, when a sudden significant gap appears between their prices, there is the highest probability that their prices will soon be close to each other again. So, you either place a Call option on the stock whose value has dropped or a Put option on the stock with a higher price.

Aggressive betting

As the name already implies, it is aggressive when you wager a big percentage of your total investment per trade, like wagering 20% per trade. Of course, the most aggressive way is to wager your whole investment on a single trade, but such is not recommended.

A famous aggressive betting strategy that is widely used by gamblers is known as the Martingale. This is where you double your wager after every loss. For example, first, you wager $10. If you lose the trade, you then wager $20. If you lose the trade again, you next wager $40, and so on... until you win a trade. When you win a trade, you go back to your initial wager of $10.

Although the Martingale looks feasible and reasonable, it is not effective in the long run.

Unfortunately, it is not surprising to experience a series of wrong investment decisions. If you get really unlucky, you may even make 10 wrong decisions in a row. There only use this strategy for a short term, and be sure to back it up with sufficient research.

Conservative betting

Your betting strategy is considered conservative if you only use a small percentage of your total investment per trade, preferably just around 1%-3%. This is good if you already have a well-developed strategy that has a high rate of success.

Corrective

This is a good strategy to use when you see a sudden and significant increase or decrease in price, especially when such price spike is not clearly justified by existing factors. In such a case, you can expect for the price to balance out by reverting to its original value prior to the price spike, or somewhat close to it.

Breakout

This strategy works well with currency pairs. When a currency pair follows a tight or close price difference, and if you see them break out, the probability is high that their prices will continue to breakout. Although they will most likely revert to their normal price range, such will take time.

Asset mastery

Pick any underlying asset of your choice. Now, find out everything that you can about your chosen asset. Follow on the news and gather as much data as you can about that asset. Do this on a regular basis, preferably daily. You will notice that the more you know about a particular asset, the better predictions you can make. This also confirms that the market does not move at random.

CHAPTER 4: KEYS TO SUCCESS

Regardless whether you only want to trade for profit or for fun, you should know the best practices that can help increase your chances of success and minimize your losses.

Money management

No matter how well developed your strategy is or how much you have increased your success rate, you can lose your investment if you fail to manage your money properly. Also, do not use the money that you need to cover your household bills and other obligations. Do not forget that options trading is a high-risk investment.

Cash out

An important part of money management is learning to cash out. Unfortunately, many traders do not cash out their profits. Although it is good to grow your funds, you should still cash out from time to time. Take note that your profits only become real when you turn them into real cash; otherwise, they are nothing but numbers on a screen and almost have no difference with demo credits. Therefore, always cash out, you do not have to cash out everything, if you want, you can just cash out 20% of your profits on a regular basis.

Research and analysis

The possibility of doing a research and analysis is what separates options trading from gambling. You need to research and be updated on the news about the businesses themselves, as well as the factors that affect business performance. When analyzing, you need to drop your personal preferences and see everything as they are. Your investment decision must be based on facts without any bias. Research is key. Remember that the outcome of every trade and the movements of the graphs are mere reflections of reality. The more you know about the economy, real people, and real businesses, the better you can make an investment decision.

Focus on the assets

Although the graphs and charts may reveal to you certain patterns, it is worth noting that such patterns are not always present. And, many times, they do not stay for so long. After all, trends are meant to change, considering that the market is alive and continues to move. When making an investment decision, be sure that you have good information on the asset that is the subject of your trade. It must be emphasized that the more you know about a particular asset, the higher is the probability of making the right investment decision.

The importance of keeping a journal

Although having a journal is not a requirement, writing a trading journal can be very helpful. You do not need to be a professional writer; you only need to be open and honest when you write your journal.

A journal will allow you to think outside the box and be a better trader. You can write anything in your journal. You can write about your new learnings, mistakes, or any adjustments that you make to your strategy. Should you decide to use a journal, be sure to update it regularly

Start small

It can be very tempting to invest a lot in a particular trade when you know that you have researched a great deal just to make that trade. However, if you are a beginner, it is best to start small and focus on increasing your success rate. First, you need to get a feel of options trading and develop your strategy. If it is your first time to trade, do not focus on making money right away. After all, once you have enough experience and confidence, you can easily increase the amount that you invest per trade. To have a good and steady profit, aim to have a success rate of at least 60%-70%.

Focus on the numbers

There are ways to somehow manipulate the stocks for a short period of time. Especially these days when you can easily and quickly send a message to the world with just a few clicks of a mouse, some people are able to make their stocks look more attractive than they really are. Unfortunately, even the media may have its own preferences and prejudices. And many so-called "experts" on options trading cannot be trusted. Therefore, you need to focus on the numbers. Words are easy to manipulate and misinterpret, but numbers do not lie. When numbers are unduly manipulated, such fraudulent scheme tends to be obvious.

Do not chase after your losses

When you engage in options trading, you should be prepared to encounter some losses. You cannot expect to make the right investment decisions all the time. Losses are part of this kind of investment. The important thing is that the outcome of all your trades results in a positive profit.

Never chase after your losses. If you do, there is a higher risk of losing more money. Instead, be positive and focus on your profits, and how to profit some more.

Most people chase after their losses by increasing the amount of their wager per trade. This is risky because your strategy may not be suited for an aggressive betting, and your funds may not be enough to handle such big wagers.

Develop your strategy
In options trading, developing a strategy simply does not end. This is because you are dealing with a

living and continuously evolving market. Therefore, you should continuously work on your strategy. It must be flexible enough to adapt to market changes and effective enough to make a decent amount of profit.

Have your own understanding of the market

True experts do not have the same strategy or share the same viewpoints all the time. They are experts because they have developed their own understanding of the market, and they can justify their views no matter how odd they may be. In the same manner, you also need to develop your own understanding of options trading and the market. In the beginning, you can rely on expert tips and advice, but soon you need to have your own way of making an investment decision. After all, nobody can get rich just by relying on expert advice. Also, out of the many people out there who claim to be "experts," only a few of them are true experts. Most of these "experts" have more losses than profits.

Practice

The only way to truly learn options trading is by actual practice. It is experience that will make you a real binary options trader. Take note that practicing does not only mean making a series of trades. In options trading, placing a trade is the easiest part. True practice means doing research and studying the various underlying assets, businesses, as well as the market behavior, among others.

Conclusion

Thank for making it through to the end of *Penny Stocks.* Let's hope it was informative and able to provide you with all of the tools you need to achieve your goals of doing well and making money with investing in penny stocks!

THANK YOU

About The Author

Hi there it's Jonathan Walker here, I want to share a little bit about myself so that we can get to know each other on a deeper level. I grew up in California, USA, and have lived there for the better part of my life. Being exposed to many different people and opportunities when I was young, it made me want to strive to become an entrepreneur to escape the rat race path that most of my peers had taken. I knew I wanted to be able to travel and experience the world the way it was meant to be seen and I've done just that. I've travelled to most places around the world and I'm enjoying every minute of it for sure. In my free time I love to play tennis and believe it or not, compose songs. I wish you all the best again in your endeavours, and may your dreams, whatever they may be, come true abundantly in the near future.